Beyond Retirement
Toward a Redirected Life

OLDER ADULT ISSUES SERIES

The Office of Older Adult Ministry of the Presbyterian
Church (U.S.A.) and Geneva Press are grateful for the
generous gifts of many individuals, congregations, and
organizations that helped make possible the publication
of this series.

Beyond Retirement
Toward a Redirected Life

HQ
1062
.M67
US

Richard L. Morgan

Published for the Office of Older Adult Ministry,
A Ministry of the General Assembly Council,
Presbyterian Church (U.S.A.)

Geneva Press
Louisville, Kentucky

Contents

Introduction

As a boy I looked forward to the annual visit of the circus, and nothing excited me more than watching the trapeze artists. Timing was essential for their act. In order to get to the next trapeze bar, they first had to let go of the bar they were holding. That bar represented security, and the next bar, the unknown. It seemed like an eternity to me when they let go and hovered for a breathless moment high above the circus dome. I breathed a sigh of relief when they safely grasped the next bar.

Retirement resembles that circus event. We let go of that first bar of our working identity, and find ourselves suspended in an unknown land before finding a new life beyond retirement. Retirement means risking a new stage of life where there are no prescribed role models to follow and no rigid rules. It means stepping out into what may be a quarter of a lifetime, and finding creative ways to make these years meaningful.

·In 1920, only 5 percent of Americans retired. The lifespan was shorter, people worked longer, and "died with their boots on." Retirement, if you had the financial resources, meant enjoying a paid mortgage, travel, and the golden wedding anniversary, while waiting to die. The person who retired at the end of the nineteenth century had only two years to live, so appropriately his or her plans focused on rest and leisure.

Advances in medical science, increased disease prevention, and improved management of chronic diseases has lengthened our lifespan by twenty-eight years. Post-retirement can last over twenty-five to thirty years; a whole new stage of life. Lydia Bronte describes this phenomenon in these words:

> But during the course of the twentieth century something has happened that has almost certainly altered the pattern of your life, most likely without realizing it. A new element has appeared that is transforming life in totally unexpected ways, the *longevity factor*. There has been a revolution regarding the length of time we live, and it is changing the future for every American.[1]

Retirement is no longer viewed as the end of life, a passive waiting for debility and death, but a whole new stage of life's journey. Surely the man or woman today who can expect twenty or more years of life would do well to design new beginnings.

The most common assumption of our Western culture, that life has a peak, a prime time, with an up and down slope on either side, is no longer valid. People do not reach their prime in the middle years, and then retire to face inevitable decline. A new third age has emerged in our time that affords limitless opportunities and challenges.

Ordinarily, there have been three approaches to retirement: (1) those who want out of the work force and can't wait to retire; (2) those who love their work and dread retirement; (3) those who don't think about it and don't plan for it. The new approach to retirement finds people making adequate financial preparations, but they are not prepared emotionally for the changes that take place.

Retirement is a major life transition, an abrupt end to one's accustomed lifestyle. It can be compared to the way a sleepwalker might feel if awakened at the edge of the roof, without knowing where he or she is, or how to get down safely. The critical search is for the significance of these bonus years, and their place in the spiritual journey that we began at childhood. How does it feel to faithfully live out the retired years?

1   Myths about Retirement

There seems to be a conspiracy of silence about how retirement really feels. Despite the abundance of retirement planning programs (which tend to focus mainly on financial and lifestyle planning), an uneasiness still marks the onset of retirement. Like most important events that mark our passage from one stage to another, retirement is surrounded by myths.

Myth #1: A successful retirement is simply a matter of financial planning. Financial planning is crucial. The number of retirees is growing, and the ratio of workers to retirees is shrinking. The coming decades promise to bring reductions in social security benefits. So deciding to retire means confronting the reality of uncertainty—can we afford to retire? But, even when retirement is affordable, there are questions about how to live these bonus years. We may have extended our years, and emptied them of their substance.

Myth #2: Joys and freedom in the retirement years may be undermined by declining health. Aging can be seen as a season with two phases: The first phase, the second summer, finds the retired person in reasonably good health. But, the second phase, the chill winter, brings declining health and increased dependence on others. So the writer of Ecclesiastes gave sound wisdom when he wrote, "Remember your creator in the days of your youth, before the days of trouble come, and the years draw near when you will say, 'I have no pleasure in them'" (Eccles. 12:1, NRSV). However, the *American Journal of Health* claims that 40 percent of all people saw their health improve with retirement, and 37 percent experienced no change.

Myth #3: Retirement and aging are synonymous. For some uninformed people retirement conjures up images of doddering old people playing shuffleboard, or watching endless television programs. Such phrases as "out to pasture," "over the hill," "on the shelf," attest to this myth. Retirement is a third stage of life, bright with new possibilities for adventure and growth, not a time of decline and stagnation.

Myth #4: Retirement is simply a time of fun and freedom. One of the popular books on retirement is titled *Retire to Fun and Freedom.* While it is true that there is more time for interests, projects, travel, and pleasure, too much can lead to stifling boredom. Edward Fischer writes:

> You will get bored and bitter unless you find something that gives meaning to life because your need for human dignity will settle for nothing less. Since mere . . . distractions are not enough, a second career will have to grow from your talents, resources, and interests. . . . You are an artist whose work is to create yourself right up to the end. No one has a right to say when that work is done—that is God's privilege.[2]

Myth #5: Being busy is the way to find happiness in retirement. Faced with this incredible new freedom from the routine of work, many retirees have trouble filling this new time. After all, there is only so much time you can spend at the pool or on the golf course. So they wallpaper the empty space with frenetic activities. Jane Thibault cites the example of "Catherine," a wealthy sixty-seven-year-old widow, who played "antique bingo," killing time to amuse herself.[3] There is a vast difference between staying active and being busy. Thomas Merton said it well: "Being too busy is a form of violence."

2   Stages of the Retirement Journey

Since retirement is a process, not a stopping place, there are discrete stages that can be identified. Gerontologist Robert Atchley has defined six stages of the retirement experience.[4] While not every person experiences each stage, the process Atchley describes makes sense. These six stages of retirement are:

1. *Preretirement.* This may be actual retirement planning, or expectations and fantasies about what retirement will be like.

2. *Honeymoon.* There is a euphoric period when retirement begins, when people "try to do all those things I never had time for before." The honeymoon period is a busy time in which the new retiree is like a child in a room full of new toys. At some point, the honeymoon ends, and life settles into a new routine.

3. *Disenchantment.* As the honeymoon begins to end, a sense of boredom and emptiness may develop. Faced with the reality that retirement is more than a long vacation, the retiree is vulnerable to depression.

4. *Reorientation.* At this stage, people begin to develop a more satisfying routine, and seek new directions

beyond a life of leisure. It is time for creative involvement in the world around them.

5. *Stability.* By this time people have developed a satisfying and relaxing routine for everyday life. They have accepted their limitations, and found new interests. Some people reach this stage directly following the honeymoon stage, some only after a painful reassessment of personal goals, and others never reach it.

6. *Termination.* According to Atchley, when a person moves from independence to dependence, and experiences crippling illnesses or debilities, the retirement phase has "terminated."

Granted, the retirement journey is a highly individual one, and each person finds his or her own way. For some, it means sitting in a rocking chair, doing nothing. A man once asked his friend what he did when he retired, and he replied, "Nothing." "What do you mean?" his friend asked. "I mean absolutely nothing, and I don't start that until dinner time." For others, it means staying busy in a whirlwind of activities. Others manage to find that vital balance between activity and creative rest.

3   Biblical Models of the Retirement Journey

In my own experience of retirement (which now spans seven years) I found a striking parallel between the exodus journey of the Israelites and retirement.[5] The paradigm is remarkably similar in its progression from bondage to deliverance to wilderness to promised land.

As the children of Israel found themselves in bondage to the Pharaoh, so I was enslaved by my addiction to work. Retirement became for me a genuine deliverance from the bondage of a demanding career. Like the Israelites, I plunged into an unknown wilderness, where there were no guidelines, and there were times when I considered going back to Egypt. The Israelites wandered three days in the wilderness of Shur without water. When they found water at Marah, it was bitter to drink. There were "bitter waters," for me in my retirement journey—times of depression, a serious, life-threatening illness, and anxiety about the future. But as Moses sweetened the waters so they could drink, I learned how these bitter experiences could be made sweet by the lessons they taught me. And all through the wilderness, like the Israelites, I learned to rely on the grace of God, not my efforts. As the Israelites moved on toward the land of promise, so I set out on a new journey of faith toward a "promised land" of new creativity and involvement. Looking back now at these seven years, I can truthfully say they were (are) the best years of my life!

Walter Brueggemann finds in the Psalms a recurring theme of orientation/disorientation/reorientation.[6] Human life goes through seasons of well-being, followed by anguish, times of hurt, suffering, and death. But this is followed by times of surprising new gifts from God, when joy breaks through the despair. Chris Zorn has shown how these themes could well be applied to the retirement experience: Preretirement, a period of *orientation*, retirement event, a period of *disorientation*, and postretirement, a time of *reorientation*.[7]

4 Tasks for the Retirement Journey

As we stand at the cusp of the twenty-first century, we face a new reality. The baby boomers will begin to retire in 2011. The institution of retirement will face a major transformation. Early retirement, which bottomed out in 1985, will become less prevalent. Most boomers will work longer in their career jobs, and then work part-time in "bridge" jobs.

Regardless of these social changes, the emotional/spiritual tasks of the retirement years remain. Retirement is a journey of the spirit—and some meaningful purpose must be created beyond retirement. Accomplishing four major tasks will help make retirement a meaningful experience:

—moving from work to redirection
—moving from center stage to cameo roles
—moving from busy-ness to soul work
—moving from independence to interdependence

Moving from Work to Redirection
Nothing can minimize the psychological adjustment of leaving the world of work for the retired life. Work provides not only a sense of worth and prestige, but valued friendships and opportunity for self-expression. The shock when that is gone cannot be measured. One CEO who retired after many years of power and authority told me, "I

went from Who's Who to Who's He?" Paul Tournier said it well: "People are so absorbed in their work, sometimes so deadened by it, their retirement takes them by surprise."[8] The golden handshakes at the retirement party can become golden handcuffs.

Although the concept of retirement is hardly mentioned in the Bible, there is one mention of it in the book of Numbers. When the Levites reached the age of fifty, they could retire and be freed from their more exacting duties. However, they did not enter a retirement community in the Sinai desert, but performed a voluntary ministry (probably mentoring younger priests) in the Tent of Meeting (Num. 8:24–26).

Jules Z. Willing compares retirement to a space capsule atop a first-stage booster rocket. The first stage, which is analogous to our work careers, provides the long journey during which we expend our energies on driving upward and forward. Success and productivity in our chosen career is our goal. But, when it has served its purpose, the booster rocket falls away, and the second stage, the capsule, comes alive. Although comparatively small, it can change directions, move on its own axis, and provide scenes of space never seen before.[9] In retirement, when the first stage has ended, and the restraints gone, we have the opportunity to discover new beginnings, and experience worlds we would never have known.

A major task of our retirement years is to let go of our work and find new directions. For some, this is incredibly difficult. Some even go back to the same job, while others look for part-time work in the same area. But God calls retirees to a new vocation. Frederick Buechner has defined vocation in this way: "The place where God calls you is the place where your deep gladness and the world's deep hunger meet."[10] Finding that place is no easy task, but when discovered, leads to new joy. Lydia Brontë believes there is a "peak creativity" time for people between the ages of fifty and seventy-five. She cites numerous examples of women and men who recorded significant achievements in those years.

Moving from Busy-ness to Soul Work
Many retired people try to cope with the new leisure time in one of two ways. Either they withdraw into passivity and vegetate, or they engage in endless leisure activities to fill the time. Nothing is sadder than to see a formerly active person sit on the porch, waiting for the mailman, or fiddling away his or her time with mindless busy-ness. Even those who retire from positions of power and visibility, people with nothing left to prove, still sense a void when their careers end. Pascal said, "The silence of these infinite spaces terrifies me." On a more worldly level, retirement means a sudden silence after the roar of work.

To fill that emptiness, many pursue what the late theologian Joseph Sittler called "geriatric shuffleboard." No longer driven by work pressures, these retirees pursue a "butterfly existence," flitting from one distraction to the next, constantly asking themselves, "What shall we do today?"

The Protestant work ethic that identified work with virtue is replaced by a retirement ethic that identifies being busy with virtue. But being too busy leads to boredom, if not depression. Often retirement communities fall into the "busy busy trap" by overscheduling activities. No wonder a group of retirees decided to leave their frenetic village and go out west, determined to form a new community and call it "Mount Rush No More!"

More affluent retired people schedule trips to faraway places. Here they can enjoy endless pleasure, and play morning, noon, and night. But this presents two problems; many retirees cannot afford such luxury, and those who can't, often travel. So for some, leisure time has become as much work as the job from which they retired.

Carl Jung referred to a morning and afternoon of life, each with different agendas. For the most part, midlife and beyond is time for greater inwardness. In the later years, it is time to accept the challenge to turn inward, seeking the rewards of meditation, reflection, and prayer. Heije Faber calls this "striking sails." The days of hoisting sails in youth have ended, and the time has come to strike sails, and slow down the pace. Retirement is a time to rest, not rush around or rust out.

Soul work also involves simplifying life. Peter Maurin has said that, "When we die, we carry in our clutched hand only what has been given away." Jesus' words to the disciples who embarked on their mission reverberate for retired persons: "Take nothing for the journey." In the last century an American tourist visited the renowned Polish Rabbi Hofetz Chaim. The affluent tourist was amazed to find the Rabbi's home only a simple room, filled only with a table, bench, and some books. "Rabbi" the American asked, "Where is your furniture?" "Where is yours?" asked the Rabbi. "Mine?" asked the puzzled tourist, "But I'm only a visitor here. I'm only passing through." "So am I," replied the Rabbi. As we live out the retirement years, it is a time to clear out the clutter, give away some of our possessions, and realize that life does not consist in "the abundance of our possessions," but in the content of our character.

Not only is simplifying life good for the soul, but it is wise preparation for the time when one faces relocation to a smaller place, or a nursing home, or for the final day when we leave this world. Not one of us would want to stand before God on that awesome day and be asked this question: "Did you become who you were supposed to be?" And it took God three days to find us, because we had so much stuff.

All retired persons would do well to practice the old Shaker song:

> 'Tis the gift to be simple,
> 'Tis the gift to be free.
> 'Tis the gift to come down where we ought to be,
> And when we find ourselves in the place just right,
> 'Twill be in the valley of love and delight.

"The place just right" is the simple life, and simplifying life for retirees is a challenge in our cosmetic, consumer-oriented society.

Moving from
Center Stage to Cameo Roles
One of the most difficult tasks of retirement is giving up being in the limelight, and switching to playing cameo roles. It is painful to be removed from center stage, and to be stripped of power. Betty Friedan has said:

> Retirement can force a restructuring of life to new purpose that does involve work in and for society, that uses men's (and women's) abilities in new ways. Such work may or may not be rewarded by money, status, or power. It is often found only after a man or woman has given up that pursuit. In fact, many of the people I interviewed who were continuing to work had lost interest in the pursuit of power.[11]

In giving up our status and power, we can discover the gospel. Formerly our identity may have centered on one of the following: I am what I do; or I am what I have; or I am what others perceive me to be. Now we can confidently affirm, I am a child of God.

While it is true that retirement empties out of a person's life her or his crutch of self-worth, it is a way to get in touch with the One who "emptied himself, taking the form of a servant" (Phil. 2:7, RSV).

Moving from
Independence to Interdependence
We are ingrained with our belief in our independence, and won't surrender it without a struggle. We need to stay in control, and feel good about ourselves to the degree that we can care for ourselves.

Emotionally, there are three different ways of relating: independently, dependently, and interdependently. Our culture generally frowns on dependence and affirms independence. One of the greatest fears about old age is increased dependence on others. Like it or not, the day may well come when we hear the words Christ spoke to Peter, "[W]hen when you were younger, you used to fasten your own belt and go wherever you wished. But when you grow old, you will stretch out your hands, and someone else will fasten a belt around you and take you where you do not wish to go" (John 21:18). It is imperative that retired persons make their own plans for relocation, and inform their adult children. This surely is a gift we bestow.

For the Christian, interdependence is the goal. We can affirm our freedom, and the freedom of each person, while at the same time recognizing the dependencies that come with aging. Interdependence means we have permission to ask for and receive help, and admit our weakness.

One major transition that comes to many retired people is moving from one's own home to a smaller home or retirement community. People leave their personal imprint on where they live, and to give that up means to surrender part of themselves. Memories get into the walls and fabric of our homes. But learning to be dependent on others, along with owning those decisions, is a major step in the retirement journey.

5 Retirement and the Marriage Relationship

The changing face of retirement also brings new challenges to couples in their later years. Men are living longer, and retiring earlier, because of burnout, cutbacks, and layoffs. Women, who may be younger, and who possibly started working later, may be hitting the peak of their careers at the time their husbands are ready to call it quits.

Some wives work longer for financial reasons, because they want or need the money, or want to build up their pensions. They may also have personal reasons—they like their jobs and colleagues and have no interest in the leisure retirement may afford. Furthermore, constant togetherness may prove to be a major issue. Formerly, it was the harassed wife who said, "Having a man around the house is like having a grand piano in the kitchen." Today it is the stay-at-home husband who says, "I married you for better or for worse—but not for lunch!"

If the husband is good at finding things to do with his leisure, or starts a second career (paid or not), the marriage suffers little. But if a husband becomes envious of his wife's career, and finds little to do outside the home, he may sink into depression.

Kathleen R. Fischer and Thomas N. Hart point to the new challenges facing two-career couples at retirement:

Retirement is the beginning of more together than we may ever have had before. And if we worked outside the home for years, it is the beginning of a whole new way of spending our days. . . . Retirement calls for yet another new marriage contract for a fresh division of responsibilities, for agreement about a mutually acceptable balance of togetherness and separateness, for new decisions about new undertakings, both individual and joint. It calls for a lot of patience with one another as we struggle to adapt to this change.[12]

Among those new decisions are: managing the care of aging relatives, finding a balance between private interests and couple activities, parenting adult children, grandparenting, and dealing with the multiple losses that inevitably come.

One thing is sure: Couples bring to the retired years the relationship built across time. Just as we bring to our aging the person we have been all our lifetime, so we bring to retirement the marriage we have built over the years. Wanda Standard, at age ninety-two, wrote the following poem celebrating her sixty-fifth wedding anniversary:

The heat of life's summer
Has spent itself
And cool winds of Autumn
Blow over seared fields.
Old memories gently fall
Like crumpled leaves;
Their day is done.
But hearts are warmer
In spite of snow
By winter's sun.[13]

6　The Changing Face of Retirement

Whatever else we may say about retirement, it is in a major state of change. The time has come for the old clichés of retirement to be forced into retirement. Perhaps the word "retirement" needs to be retired. Let's call it reengagement, or redirection, or the next chapter.

For most people retiring in this decade there will be no major changes. But no one can predict accurately what lies ahead in the twenty-first century. The baby boomers and Generation Xers will change the face of what we now know as retirement. Some will surely be more affluent than today's retirees. Some will start new careers for pleasure, while others will continue to work because they must. Unless some fundamental policy changes are forthcoming, more baby boomers will be spending their later years working just to make ends meet. Most will move in and out of varied careers, and will live longer and healthier lives than their parents' generations did.

Lydia Bronte wrote:

> More than fifty years after it became an American institution, the concept of retirement is going through a period of transition and realignment. Our idea of retirement as the culmination of the American dream—a period of leisure at the end of adult life when one is free to do as

he or she pleases without involvement in work—has become blurred. It is evolving into another, albeit one that has not yet achieved a definite shape.[14]

In that sense, retirement parallels the Christian life. For this life is neither static, nor fixed on the past. It is always moving forward toward what is yet to be. John Burton is a "retired" Presbyterian minister, and is one of my role models of creative retirement. Some years ago he shared a poem with me, and it still captures the restless spirit of these redirected years. In many ways it reflects the retirement journey.

I must make my way to the mountains and find a path
    to the sea,
let the far and silent places become a part of me,
for my world has grown so small that there is no room
    at all
for my spirit, twisting, turning to be free.

I must dwell awhile in the desert, or walk beside a lake,
for something asleep within me is trying to come awake,
and my life has dwindled down to a single, little town
and my spirit is twisting, turning to be free.

I will go beyond horizon, trace a western star,
rest my eyes on a prairie reaching wide and far.
For this journey I have no guide save what seems to be
inside, where my spirit is twisting, turning to be free.

I may come once more to freedom in this same, familiar
    street,
break out of the bondage if I really meet
those who, knowing me, have eyes with which to see
my spirit twisting, turning to be free.[15]

In the opening lines of his classic novel A *Tale of Two*

Cities, Charles Dickens writes, "It was the best of times, it was the worst of times . . . , it was the season of Light, it was the season of Darkness, it was the spring of hope, it was the winter of despair, we had everything before us, we had nothing before us. . . ."[16] Retirement can be either the best or the worst of times.

Whatever else may be said about this new stage of life's journey, it is no longer that short period between frailty and death. It is a third stage of life, bright with hopes and possibilities. It is a time to find that creative balance between involvement and solitude. It is a time to keep growing, following the example of the apostle Paul, who late in his life wrote to the Philippians, "Not that I have already obtained this or already reached the goal; but I press on to make it my own, because Christ Jesus has made me his own. Beloved, I do not consider that I have made it my own; but this one thing I do: forgetting what lies behind and straining forward to what lies ahead, I press on toward the goal for the prize of the heavenly call of God in Christ Jesus" (Phil. 3:12–14). Retirement is an opportunity, not a fate; it is an enrichment, not a diminishment. And we can live these years with courage and faith.

7 Planning a Creative Retirement

Retirement is a major life transition, and needs careful planning if one is not just to *go* through it, but *grow* through it. Some people make their plans with a financial counselor, but we have already recognized that there is more to planning retirement than getting our financial portfolio in order.

A helpful way to anticipate your retirement years is to reflect now on those years, and get a sense of what they might mean. Carol Spargo Pierskalla took a leave of three months in 1989 and reflected on what her retirement years might be like. Later, she journaled her experiences in a book published by Judson Press, *Rehearsal for Retirement*.[17] She simulated what it would be like for a woman who finds herself aging and alone. So, for three months, she left her home and her husband and assumed the identity of an older woman, living alone, on a fixed income. The wisdom she gained through reflection and experience enriched her life and prepared her for the retirement years. Some of the exercises in the rest of this book will help you reflect on your life, assess your attitudes toward retirement, and prepare for those years.

Another helpful way to plan a creative retirement is to organize a group of people in your congregation who are either planning for retirement or are already retired. The following guide would have greater value in a group setting, where ideas, experiences, and fears could be exchanged.

In a group setting, ask each person to pick a partner and sit next to him or her. Have everyone fill out the card (following the directions) and share the information with his or her partner. When the group reconvenes, have each person introduce his or her partner to the group.

Directions:

1. Write your first name in large letters in the center of the card.
2. In the upper-left-hand corner of the card, briefly describe your first job.
3. In the upper-right-hand corner, describe your greatest career success.
4. In the lower-left-hand corner, write one word that comes to mind when you hear the word retirement.
5. In the lower-right-hand corner, write what you believe will be your greatest challenge in retirement.

First Job		Career Success
	First Name	
Retirement is:		
_____		Challenge

Retirement Attitude Inventory

(Check the items that reflect your attitude about retirement)

___1. I can't wait to retire and do exactly as I please.

___2. I don't want to stop working; I love my work and my colleagues.

___3. I won't waste my time with retirement planners. All they do is waste your time.

___4. When I retire, I'll be so busy with the hobbies I neglected that I won't have time to get bored or depressed.

___5. It's much better to retire when your health is good.

___6. I worry that caring for my aging parents and my own needs will exhaust my funds.

___7. I seldom worry about where I'll live when I retire. Just trust the Lord.

___8. Since so much of my identity is tied up with my work, I admit I dread being "retired."

___9. If all goes as expected, I'll inherit enough money from my family to have a comfortable retirement.

___10. When I retire and do volunteer work, it will be on my terms.

___11. All I want to do when I retire is have fun. I agree with the old saying "Life is two periods of play surrounding forty years of work."

___12. I don't want to be a burden to my children, so I am planning my future wisely; I have made a down payment in a retirement community, and have nursing-home insurance.

___13. When I think about the status of the economy, the uncertainty of social security and Medicare, retirement scares me.

____14. Leaving my work will be a major transition; but I intend to find a second career and be useful as long as I can.

____15. I really haven't given much thought to retirement. I'll worry about that when the time comes.

____16. God not only calls us to a specific work, but to a lifelong vocation.

The following profiles are actual stories of retired persons. Which of these profiles either describes your retired experience, or what you anticipate retirement to be? (If you are in a group, discuss which of the following profiles express your feelings about retirement).

> I've worked in an office for twenty years since my divorce from Jeff. Recently, my boss told me that I *had* to retire at age sixty-five, which will be this year. I really need to work longer, and feel I am still proficient and capable at my job. But I have no choice. I worry that my small pension and social security will not pay the bills. I'll have to look for another part-time job, but who wants to hire an "old" woman? Right now I just don't have the desire or energy to do anything.
>
> —Mary, *retiring from her secretarial position*

> It seemed strange at first, not wearing that suit and tie, and lugging that briefcase to the office. I felt out of sorts for a while. But later I loved getting away from the pressure. As an attorney, I was not allowed to make any mistakes. Now I can make mistakes and not worry about it. I enjoy quality time with my family, and feel better than I have for ten years.
>
> —Steven, *retired attorney*

We really looked forward to retiring from our jobs. We made a lot of plans to travel and take pleasure trips. We had signed up for a cruise to the Bahamas. Then Debbye had a stroke, and I spend most of my time caring for her.

—*Donovan, husband of Debbye*

You know, it took me twenty minutes to adjust to being retired. It was such a relief not to go to the church office every day. I feel like Simon Peter; an angel has released me from prison! No more late phone calls, family crises, irritated parishioners. I really enjoy sleeping late, walking the dog, reading the paper, watching old movies, and playing golf.

—*Frank, retired pastor*

Retirement? That's for lazy people. The Bible never mentions retirement, and Christians never retire from the Lord's work. I loved my job, and when they retired me, I took another job and plan to work until I drop. After all, God never retires, so should I? I can't believe these people who sit on the porch and wait for the mailman. I stay busy . . . and tired all the time.

—*Art, retired electrician*

All my life I have worked with little children. I taught elementary school for forty years, but when my husband got sick, I took care of him until he died. After that, I got real depressed and slept a lot. Finally my pastor suggested I do some volunteer work at our Learning Center. It has turned my life around! I give ten hours a week, and read stories to the children. They call me "Grandma." It keeps me going, and gives me a reason to get out of bed in the morning.

—*Lucy, retired reading specialist*

I am a single woman who taught school for thirty years. After my divorce, I retired and decided I wasn't ready to stay home. I began a second career, went to the Seminary, and, after graduation, accepted a call as an associate pastor of a downtown church. I feel a "call" to do older adult ministry, and really look forward to this new venture in my life.

—*MaryBeth, retired teacher, redirected pastor*

I planned my retirement well. I have enough money to do whatever I want. I have booked passage on several cruises, rented and equipped an office where I work on my investments. So, why do I feel depressed? My children are so wrapped up in their own lives that they have little time for me. When I meet people and they ask me what I do, I used to say "I am a bank executive." Instead, now I say "I am retired," and I see their faces change. I guess I was what I did, and now I do nothing, so I am nothing.

—*Howard, retired bank vice president*

Since his retirement, Chuck follows me around the house and won't let me out of his sight. He monitors my every move, and has even invaded my kitchen. When he's not hovering over me, or under my feet, he sits with that almighty remote control and drives me crazy flipping from one channel to the next. If he doesn't find something to do, I think I'll lose my mind.

—*Jane, wife of "retired" Chuck*

8 Retirement Is a Spiritual Journey

Elizabeth Harbottle, Chairman of the Christian Council of Aging in the United Kingdom, describes the spiritual crisis of retirement as an exodus experience:

> It is a desert place; a place to develop spiritual strength, a place for life review and discovery of resources, skills and experiences built up over a life-time; it is a place of suffering, of facing regrets of the past, failures and missed opportunities, a time to feel the pointlessness of the journey so far or to fear the traumas that may lie ahead. The apparently empty desert, seemingly useless and impractical like prayer, can like prayer be the most creative and fruitful. It is a watershed, a time to try out new things and shed others. It is a time to get to know oneself better.[18]

You may recall earlier that my own retirement journey was also likened to the exodus experience. If you are simply reflecting on your own retirement journey, how would the following events of the exodus relate to your story?

From bondage to freedom _____

_____

Going back to Egypt _____

_____

Bitter waters and murmuring _____

_____

The wilderness _____

_____

Crossing the Jordan _____

_____

Possessing the land _____

_____

Christians believe that God has called us to use our talents as long as we have breath. There is no retirement from the service of God. The biblical world has no concept of retirement as it has been established in modern society.

Vocation means a lifelong calling. We may retire from a profession, or a job, or a series of jobs. But we need to continue to seek ways of using our talents to serve God through serving others. Henry Simmons claims that our American pragmatic approach to life classifies retired persons as has-beens, who, when stripped of their work, forfeit their identity. The retired years are not for the side-lines, but for vital involvement in life. How, then, can a Christian discern God's call for the retirement years?

Although each person must find his or her own way, the possibilities for service beyond retirement are limitless. Each of us, if we are to discover that special calling for the later years, must do what Thomas Moore calls "soul work." He writes:

> The ultimate work . . . is an engagement with soul, responding to the demands of fate and tending the details of life as it presents itself. We may get to the point where our external labors and the *opus* of the soul is one

and the same, inseparable. Then the satisfactions of our work will be deep and long lasting, undone neither by failures nor flushes of success.[19]

Those words ring true not only for the working career, but for the retirement years when our soul work can become the ministry we do.

Read the following poem by presbyterian minister John David Burton, and discuss with your group what feelings it evokes in you.

Once Again, Dime Time

On Saturdays, in 1929, I walked up and down
in front of a movie house in Texarkana, Texas,
in my hand a dime hard-earned in cottonfield
or candling eggs on a neighbor's farm,
As I walked I wondered.

"Shall I spend the dime to see Tom Mix and
Tarzan of the Apes?"

Sometimes I saved the dime, went off play
on feed sacks at the general store where
the family was shopping until we loaded into
the black Dodge touring car for going home.
When I did go to the picture show, I stayed through twice. It
cost no more and made me think the dime well spent.

Now, half a century later, I must decide how to spend
not a dime, but time—the time left of my life. . . .
What shall I buy with time? More of what I have purchased
up to now, regard[ed] by many as a known and
reliable quantity in a changing world? With what time
left, I can buy some more of that, and all will say, "Amen."

Or is there something else to buy with what time is left,
a moment of joy, adventure equal to that movie house
of long ago?
Is there some friend to see, to tell of love, or
a final follow-through with children for which
to use what time is left to me?

On Saturdays long ago, I made the choice to spend or save.
Now, each fleeting day I must choose what
to do with hurrying time.
It is "dime time" once again.[20]

As you plan your "dime time" in the retirement years,
how will you spend your time? _____

_____

_____

_____

_____

_____

_____

9   Final Reflections

The intention of this book was to help you view retirement as a journey, not a destination. The financial issues of retirement were deliberately sidestepped. Although crucial to a good retirement, the spiritual/emotional issues are more important. Reflect on the following words about retirement from different writers, and then reflect on your own retirement:

> Life begins at retirement—not because your job is finally behind you, but because the world is opening up before you, and you've prepared yourself for your debut.
>
> —*Helen Hayes*

> A second career . . . a free career . . . has no set specifications, no contract, no hierarchy, no age-limit, no routine, no fixed wage tied to an obligation to work. . . . It has nothing to do with a second job. . . . It is a situation where the only responsibility an individual has is to himself.
>
> —*Paul Tournier*

> Ultimately, a successful retirement is not contingent on how many stocks a person owns, or whether it is possible to travel to exotic locations, but rather on living with inner peace regardless of external situations that threaten our lives.
>
> —*Robert Veninga*

. . . It is time to redefine not only my retirement, but retirement for women. It is only with a new definition that we may see more clearly the priorities, options, and opportunities of this important phase of life. With this new definition, I have begun to view retirement as a beginning, not as an end. It is not necessarily a time to stop working, but a time of change, perhaps a time to add a new context to one's life, an opportunity for a new future. . . . When I view the future this way, the thirty years that are statistically probable for me open up with possibilities.

—*Diane Cort-VanArsdale*

The moment of retirement itself may be a shocking encounter with the transition about to be made. . . . For the unprepared, for whose creativity and involvement in work has been of major importance and whose identity is largely derived from that work, there can be a bitter and deprived feeling of being expelled and depreciated.

—*Erik H. Erikson, Joan M. Erikson,*
and Helen Q. Kivnick

There is no such thing as retirement in terms of the purpose of God; the whole idea of retirement at age 65 is eroding, dehumanizing, destroying the human spirit so that those who have not reached age 65 are already living in fear and trepidation. God calls us to live life with Him as co-creators, co-workers in the reshaping and renewing of human history toward the new creation . . . and that calling is never completed until the day He calls us to live with Him.

—*Jitsuo Morikawa*

Eight years ago I kept journals of my years leading up to retirement, and then I continued to write during those first months of this incredible journey. I wanted to help people understand the emotional and spiritual issues of retirement. The result was my book *I Never Found That Rocking Chair* (Upper Room Books, 1993), which was like a letter to retired people. Now, six years later into the retirement journey, somewhere between the wilderness and the land of promise, I can add this postscript to that original letter:

—*There is no such thing as "retirement" from ministry.* Our calling is never completed until this life ends; so in these extended years we need to continue to listen for God's call.

—*There is an alternative rhythm, a vital balance in these years.* We can find a creative balance between activity and rest. Although "being" is more important than "doing," we still need something to do.

—*We learn to turn away from the familiar past in order to embrace new possibilities.* That does not mean we throw away our experiences that we have earned throughout life, but that we explore new ways to use our gifts for the service of God.

Every day I am more and more convinced we should retire the word "retirement" and replace it with another concept. Perhaps *refirement* is the word. Our steps may be slower, our hair whiter, our wrinkles all too apparent, but the fire is still there! So the journey continues for me . . . and you.

Notes

1. Lydia Bronte, *The Longevity Factor* (New York: HarperCollins, 1993), xv.

2. Edward Fischer, *Life in the Afternoon: Good Ways of Growing Older* (Mahwah, N.J.: Paulist Press, 1987), 22.

3. Jane Marie Thibault, *A Deepening Love Affair: The Gift of God in Later Life* (Nashville: Upper Room Books, 1993), 13.

4. Robert Atchley, *Social Forces and Aging* (Belmont, Calif.: Wadsworth Publishers, 1987), 172–74.

5. Richard L. Morgan, *I Never Found That Rocking Chair: God's Call at Retirement* (Nashville: Upper Room Books, 1993).

6. Walter Brueggemann, *The Message of the Psalms: A Theological Commentary* (Minneapolis, Minn.: Augsburg Publishing House, 1984).

7. Christopher E. Zorn, "What Next? God's Call at Retirement" (Master's thesis, 1994), 33.

8. Paul Tournier, *Learn to Grow Old* (New York: Harper & Row, 1971), 13.

9. Jules Z. Willing, *The Reality of Retirement: The Inner Experience of Becoming a Retired Person* (New York: William Morrow & Co., 1981), 219–20.

10. Frederick Buechner, *Wishful Thinking* (New York: Harper & Row, 1973), 84.

11. Betty Friedan, *The Fountain of Age* (New York: Simon & Schuster, 1993), 225.

12. Kathleen R. Fischer and Thomas N. Hart, *Promises to Keep: Developing the Skills of Marriage* (Mahwah, N.J.: Paulist Press, 1991), 173.

13. Used by permission of Wanda Standard.

14. Bronte, *The Longevity Factor*, 317.

15. "Amplius," from *Naked in the Street: Selected Poems of John David Burton*. Used by permission of the author.

16. Charles Dickens, *A Tale of Two Cities* (Garden City, N.Y.: International Collectors Library, n.d.), 9.

17. Carol Spargo Pierskalla, *Rehearsal for Retirement: My Journey into the Future* (Valley Forge, Pa.: Judson Press, 1991).

18. Elizabeth Harbottle, unpublished material, quoted in Michael Butler and Ann Orbach, "Being Your Age: Pastoral Care for Older People" (London: SPCK, 1993), 54–55.

19. Thomas Moore, *Care of the Soul* (New York: HarperCollins, 1992), 185.

20. "Once Again, Dime Time," from *Naked in the Street: Selected Poems of John David Burton*. Used by permission of the author.

Further Reading

Bronte, Lydia. *The Longevity Factor*. New York: HarperCollins, 1993.

Deane, Barbara. *Getting Ready for a Great Retirement: A Planning Guide*. Colorado Springs, Colo.: NavPress, 1992.

Fetridge, Guild A. *The Adventure of Retirement: It's about More than Just Money*. New York: Prometheus Books, 1994.

Gross, Deborah. *Beyond the Gold Watch: Living in Retirement*. Louisville, Ky.: Westminster John Knox Press, 1994.

Morgan, Richard L. *I Never Found That Rocking Chair: God's Call at Retirement*. Nashville: Upper Room Books, 1993.

Otterbourg, Robert K. *Kiplinger's Retire and Thrive*. Washington, D.C.: Kiplinger Washington Editors, Inc., 1995.

Pierskalla, Carol Spargo. *Rehearsal for Retirement: My Journey into the Future*. Valley Forge, Pa.: Judson Press, 1992.

Small, Dwight H. *Letting Go and Moving On*. Grand Rapids: Baker Book House, 1993.

Veninga, Robert L. *Your Renaissance Years*. Boston: Little, Brown & Company, 1991.

Willing, Jules Z. *The Reality of Retirement: The Inner Experience of Being a Retired Person*. New York: William Morrow & Company, 1991.